Writing about fauna in newspapers of Cuba and Puerto Rico

ALBERTO R. ESTRADA

ACKNOWLEDGMENTS

My thanks to everyone who helped me with the process of writing and publishing this handful of articles in Cuba and Puerto Rico..

1 Introduction

The nature conservation is not possible if humans do not receive adequate ecological education. Education, in most societies worldwide, leaves out of its contents most basic information that any child needs to grow to learn about their natural environment and understand that they are an inseparable part of a whole.

Perhaps this is because since humans stop being a bunch of wild species of apes, we begin to see the rest of nature as something that was already there, for our welfare and dominion, something to be used and subordinate to our whim. Something created to satisfy our vital needs, or give us pleasure or fear.

In many societies, the dissemination of scientific issues about the nature, appears sporadically in the press, radio, television, online and in the literature, generally in spaces granted to satisfy a minority composed of biologists, enthusiasts of the plants and pets, environmentalists, ecologists and other dreamers.

In my personal experience as a communicator on themes of nature, I faced many difficulties to find spaces for publication both in my own country and in exile. Almost

1

no media was interested in something that had not been written by a journalist, and in many cases, to find an opportunity for publication, manuscripts and titles were handled by editors that in many cases, distorted into something the message carrying the original article.

In this book, I wanted to meet six articles published in newspapers and not scientific journals, in Havana, Cuba and San Juan, Puerto Rico, in a 19-year period beginning in 1985, and ends in 2004. The works deal with species of the fauna of Cuba and Puerto Rico. In some cases, the information they contain is untimely or has changed, for that reason at the end of each article, such discrepancies are discussed. I have used the original version of the manuscript of each item that was submitted to the drafting of the media outlet who published it, making slight modifications.

2 Small snake with four legs?

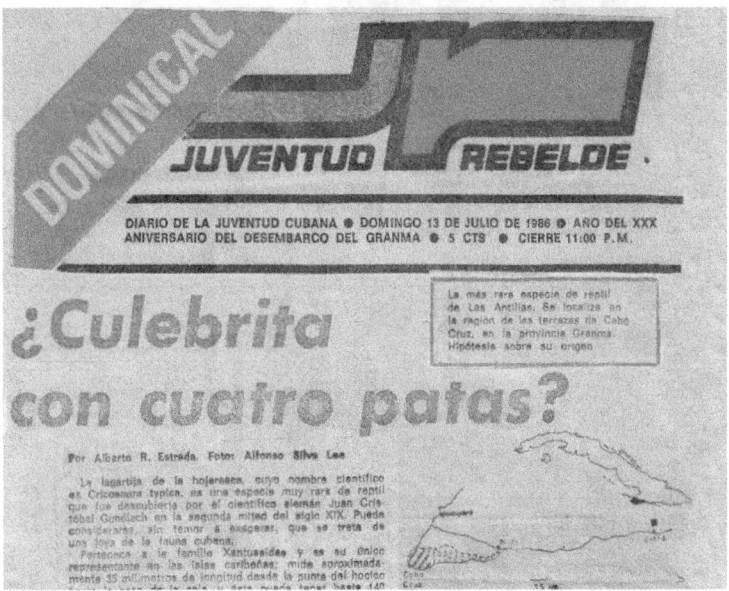

Published on Sunday, July 13, 1986 in the daily Juventud Rebelde, Havana, Cuba.

In July 1986, and through my colleague and friend Giraldo Alayón, I made contact with the persons in charge of posting an occasional brief column on popular science, in the daily Juventud Rebelde in Havana, Cuba. So this article was my first contribution to the important task of disseminating, to the public, curiosities unknown by the common citizen, about the fauna of Cuba.

By that time, I was part of the group of professionals who worked in the National Enterprise of Protection of Flora and Fauna, that was devoted to the design and management of the protected areas in the whole of the Cuban archipelago and was investigating an interesting reptile that inhabits in the region of Cabo Cruz, in the former province of Oriente (Granma today) where a National Park would be established.

The Cuban Night Lizard, whose scientific name is *Cricosaura typica*, is a very rare species of reptile that was discovered by the German scientist Juan Cristobal Gundlach, in the second half of the nineteenth century. You can be considered, without fear of exaggeration, which is a jewel of the Cuban fauna.

It belongs to the family Xantusiidae and its sole representative in the Caribbean islands. Measures approximately 35 mm in length from the tip of its snout to the base of the tail, and this can have up to 140 mm of length.

The shape of the body, rather than a lizard, reminiscent of a small snake, is more or less cylindrical, the head is wedge-shaped, is short in relation to the rest of the body and she is highlight great smooth scales and the small eyes devoid of eyelids. Its four limbs are short, equipped with five fingers fine armed with claws.

The queue of this reptile, in its base and in good part of its length, maintains the same thickness of the body. The back is an earthy brown color with some clear longitudinal lines that run through its side. The underparts are yellow-orange very bright.

Another character that makes us think in a small snake with four legs is due to the way it moves combining the movement of their short legs with the winding movements of its body and tail.

Night Lizard *Cricosaura typica* (Photo: A. Silva Lee)

Where do they live, and what are they feeds?

Cricosaura typica, unlike most lizards of Cuba, is not characterized by their abilities to climb. It spends most of its time in the soil and how its common name in Spanish (Lagartija de hojarasca) points out, in the leaf litter, inside of which is moved with surprising skill and without revealing its steps, to which also contributes the coloring that makes it almost indistinguishable in the middle of the wide variety of brown tones of the dead leaves on the forest floor.

We must clarify that it is not any type of forest that serves as a home to this peculiar reptile, since only it can be found in deciduous forests and coastal scrub typical of the marine terraces, which are located in the region of Cabo Cruz, Granma province. These forest formations grow in soils with abundant limestone outcrops (dogtooth) and soil is red.

Precisely the rocks play an important role in the life of this species, because *Cricosaura typica* uses them as refuge If one of these rocks is removed, these rocks are virtually planted in loose soil and moist, surrounded by a sea of leaf litter, if one of these rocks is removed, can be discovered an individual slip through one of the many entrances to the winding tunnel that constitutes its shelter.

The Cuban Night Lizards usually remain during the day in the shelters and are most active at night when look for food, which basically is constituted by ants and small beetles that eat in large quantities.

Why this reptile is the rarest of the West Indies?

The most recent geological findings concerning the origin of our archipelago, and the evidence on the origin of our fauna, indicate that the arrival of the groups of animals from the continent, through various ways, not must have occurred prior to the middle Eocene (40 million years ago approximately). However, it is possible that some earlier colonizers have survived to the constant fluctuations of the ocean level and to the movements of ascent and descent of the tectonic plates.

Such colonizers were exposed to conditions of isolation and subsequently very drastic could diversify and disperse from the middle Eocene. *Cricosaura typical* has no kinship or relationship with any other group of living or extinct reptiles (back to the late middle Eocene), in Cuba or in West Indian lands. On the other hand, shares an extinct common ancestor genus with two living night lizard genera: *Klauberina* of the Channel Islands in California and *Xantusia* of Central America. This ancestor lived in the early Eocene.

The hypothesis about the origin of this rare reptile is drawn to the possibility of an accidental arrival of groups related to the ancestral form in the early Eocene times before that the Cuban archipelago acquire its contemporary settings. It is possible that these populations have been isolated in territories emerged evolving into what we know today as the current genus *Cricosaura*. But what is there is only this genus in Cuba? There is no more species of *Cricosaura*? How arrived in the territory where is currently distributed that is much more recent than the arrival of the ancestral populations? These and many other questions waiting for answers.

Also in the Sierra Maestra

Dr. Luis F. de Armas, a specialist in scorpions of the Institute of Ecology and Systematics of the CITMA collected a male night lizard, at the time it was identified as *Cricosaura typica*, during his research in the vicinity of Uvero, Sierra Maestra in 1972.

The surprising thing about the finding is that the habitat in Uvero not have a great similarity to the habitat of Cabo Cruz. The discovery takes place at 120 km to the east of Cabo Cruz at an elevation ranging between 300 and 400 meters above sea level. The previous distribution known does not exceed 200 meters of elevation.

Luis V. Moreno from the same institution, collected a female *Cricosaura* in the same region in which the Dr. de Armas had found his specimen in 1972. When comparing the two copies of the zone of Uvero with copies of Cabo Cruz, arose the hypothesis that this new population could correspond to a new species different from C. *typica*, especially taking into account the ecological differences between the region of Cabo Cruz and Uvero. These arguments seemed to provide a test case in favor of the hypothesis before exposed on the origin of the genus *Cricosaura*.

Will be assured the future of this rare reptile?

There are not many data that the bibliography collects on this species. Between the date of its discovery in 1863 and 1960 had been briefly studied by only five authors. Best known is its original and current distribution. It was originally distributed throughout the forested region to the southeast and south of Niquero being the, taking as limit the coastal scrub to the west and the south in an area covering about 200 square kilometers.

Today the development of agriculture and forestry have reduced the originals limits of available habitat for this species. Only known its presence in an area of 50 square km in the vicinity of Cabo Cruz. The remaining 50 square kilometers of its original distribution, a bit further to the north are now deforested by the expansion of agriculture and other land uses.

There are approximately 100 square kilometers in which the scientists are studying the possibility of its existence. This territory extends to the east of Cabo Cruz to near Pilón. The competent institutions have included this territory within **Desembarco del Granma National Park,** which would be preserved for our people the rest of humanity the countless treasures historical, archaeological, and natural that the region contained. As we see, the future of *Cricosaura typica* is secured.

Comments

After several Cuban - American Herpetological expeditions that explored the region of Cabo Cruz and Sierra Maestra between the 1991 and 1994 summers, the known distribution of C. *typica* was permanently extended. Until 1991, it was considered that their populations were highly restricted to areas not far from South of Belic and the vicinity of Cabo Cruz.

Today it is known that its distribution covers all the forests of the plateau of Cabo Cruz including the southern slope of the Sierra Maestra from Mareón to Uvero. The existence of a second species that is associated with the record of a specimen collected in Uvero was also discarded. None of the localities where populations were detected rises more than 200 m above the sea level.

A couple collected during said expeditions was kept in captivity for 20 months. At the end of a year the female began to dig depressions in the soil of the terrarium in which was kept and fed together an adult male. Three eggs were deposited by the female in the most humid zone of the terrarium. All three were partially buried. From the first egg laid to the third, spent 90 days approximately. The first eggs not hatched, but the remaining two took between 52 and 57 days to hatch. The total length of the newborns was 21 and 20 mm respectively, and the length of their tails was 30 and 26 mm respectively.

Egg partially buried of *C. typica* (Photo: A. R. Estrada)

Adult individual of Cricosaura typica
(Photo: A. R. Estrada)

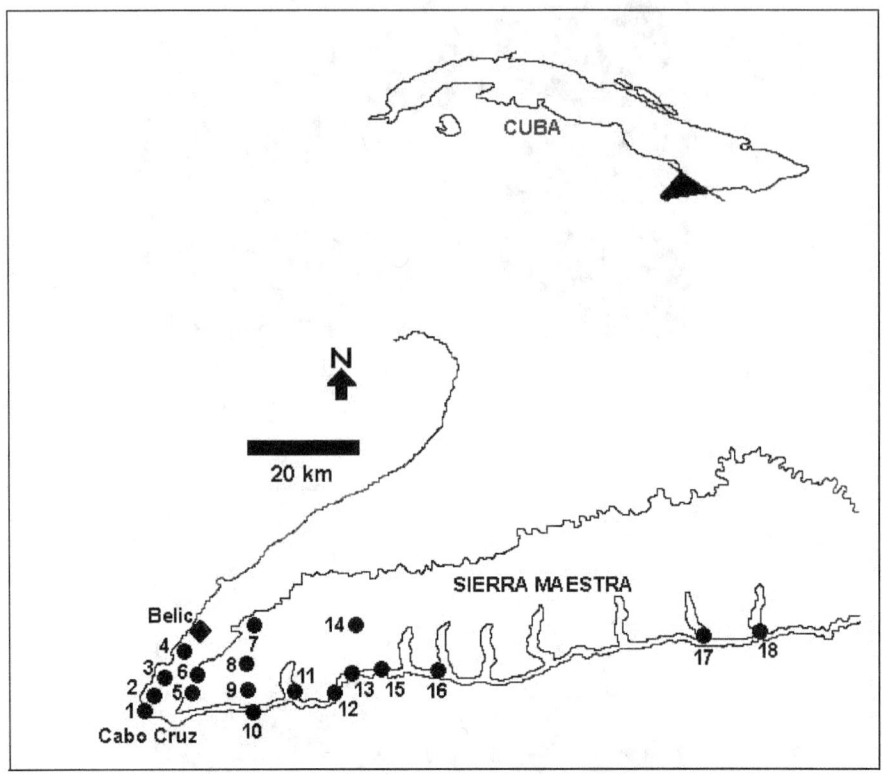

Geographic distribution of *C. typica:* Granma province: 1.- Hoyo de la Campana, Cabo Cruz, (5 m s.n.m.); 2.- Monte Gordo, (40 m s. n. m.); 3.- Vereón, (45 m s .n. m.); 4.- Playa Las Coloradas, (al n. m.); 5.- Currín; 6.- Agua Fina; 7.- Bosque Castillo; 8.- 1.1 km al N de Algría de Pío (200 m s .n. m.); 9.- Bajada al Pesquero de la Alegría (200 m s. n. m.); 10.- Pesquero de la Alegría 11.- 2.4 km al SE de Ojo del Toro (50 m s. n. m.); 12.- Caleta Media Luna; 13.- Punta de Piedra (5 m s. n. m.); 14.- Alto de Mareón (150-180 m s. n. m.); 15.- Marea del Portillo; 16.- Camarón Grande (35 m s. n. m.). Santiago de Cuba, province:17.- Boca del Río la Mula; 18.- Uvero.

3 About the tiny snakes with four legs

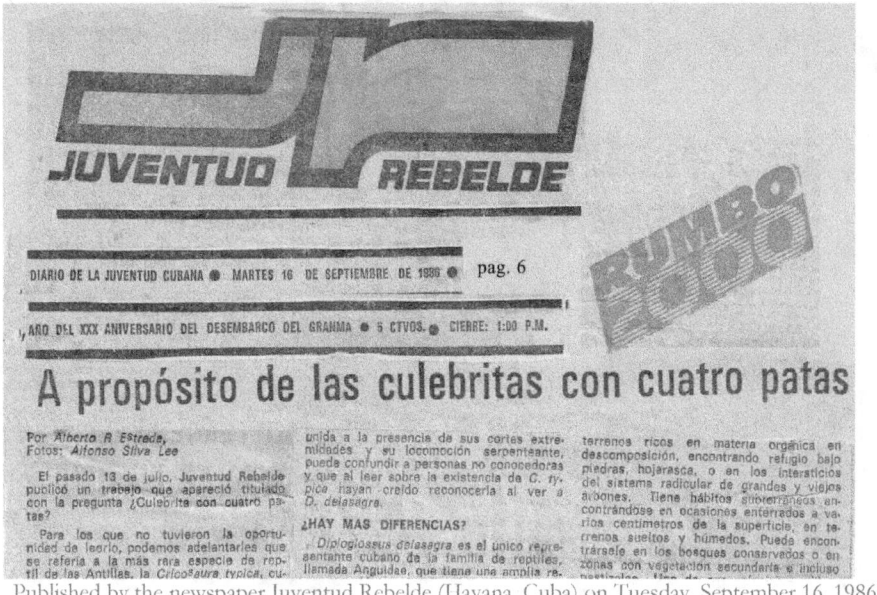

Published by the newspaper Juventud Rebelde (Havana, Cuba) on Tuesday, September 16, 1986.

The following article was a sequel to the previous. The confusion generated by the way in which the work appeared entitled, attracted some interest of the public and managers of columns in popular science of Juventud Rebelde, by the "four-legged snakes". It was so much interest that I telephoned the newspaper to ask for a job that more girl on the subject and give answers to the people about the controversy that arose. Thus sees the light of my second article on this evening newspaper.

Last July 13, Juventud Rebelde published work appeared titled with the question: Small snake with four legs?

For those who did not have the opportunity to read it, we can already tell you that concerned "the rarer reptile species of the Antilles" (as it says in the subtitle of the article), the *Cricosaura typica*, whose common name is Cuban Night Lizard (Lagartija de la Hojarasca in Spanish). It is true that in the brief description is made of rare reptile, compared its shape with a small snake which he had grown very small four legs and is no less true that this detail used in the heading of the article has attracted a mixture of interest and confusion in our readers and many have been the letters we have received and also phone calls. Also some specialists of the Academy of Sciences have received communications from people who claim to have seen the rare animal in locations such as Gibara in Holguín province; Bueycito in the Sierra Maestra, Granma province; San Nicolas in Havana and many other localities of the island. This is a remarkable fact in the sense that he had raised that *Cricosaura typica* had a restricted distribution in the vicinity of Cabo Cruz.

Small Snake With Four Legs, *Diploglossus nigropunctatus* (described as *Celestus. delasagra. nigropunctata* by Barbour and Shreve 1937) according to the original illustration of the holotype by EN Fisher

Are these reptiles throughout Cuba?

This question has a twofold answer: no and yes. No, because the specimens reported by readers in myriad localities of the country, does not belong to the species treated in the article of July 13. And yes, because this is another Cuban species of reptile that lives in all the territory of Cuba and the Isle of Youth (formerly Isla de Pinos). But it is necessary to make it clear that the readers were not misguided, since *Diploglossus delasagra* (scientific name of the species) has the appearance of a snake with four legs and with more likeness because its size is more like a small snake. This species, as we already pointed out lives in all of Cuba and its cylindrical body and its tail also cylindrical and very robust as a continuation of its body, with the presence of their four tiny limbs and his winding walk, may confused to people not familiar with reptiles, having read the article on *C. typica* create fun observing and not to *D. delasagra*.

Are there more differences?

Diploglossus delasagra is the only Cuban representative of the family Anguidae, which has a large representation in the West Indies and throughout Latin America, and especially the genus *Diploglossus* has about 13 known species to the islands of the Caribbean Sea and some more to Central and South America and its evolutionary history is much more recent and clearly linked to groups of primitive anguids that colonized the islands of the West Indies from the mainland territories. For its part *C. typica*, is the sole representative of the family Xantusiidae in the insular Caribbean and its genus and species are unique to Cuba. Although the shape of the body, already mentioned, it is similar in the two species, there are profound differences in the shape and the arrangement of the scales, and what is most obvious is the difference in size: *D. delasagra* has a total length (body and tail) average of 17.7 cm, while the dimensions of C. typica are 7.5 cm. As can be seen *D. delasagra* is more than twice the small *C. typica*.

There are also differences in the colorful: the first is brown or almost black, or with

13

a brown-olive tone in the dorsal parts, with patches of brown or black dark brown. It is also distinguished by a black stripe down the sides from behind the eyes up to the tail. While *C. typica* is colored brown-reddish in their dorsal parts and a ventral coloration orange.

Another difference is that *D. delasagra* is not considered a species threatened with extinction, although their populations in certain places are not abundant and for its part *C. typica* due to reduced distribution itself is threatened of extinction.

D. delasagra was described by Cocteu in the in the Physics, Politics and Natural History of the Island of Cuba, published by Ramón de la Sagra between 1838 and 1839 and was named with the common name of "Four-legged Small Snake" (Culebrita de Cuatro Patas in Spanish).

Other data on the four-legged Small Snake

Since we are talking about this species, which has been protagonist of a little confusion, we will give you some interesting information on their biology. Living mostly buried in the upper layers of soil very rich in organic matter in decomposition, also finding refuge under stones, leaf litter or in the interstices of the root system of large and old trees. Habits has found underground sometimes buried several inches of the surface in loose and moist soil. It can be found in well preserved forests or in areas with secondary vegetation and even pastures. One of their favorite shelters are the rotten trunks of fallen trees. At sites such as these was discovered by Dr. P. J. Darlington in 1936 to more than 900 m over the sea level in the mountains north of Imías (Guantánamo province), an adult female with its clutch of with 6 white eggs. This is the only known report of reproduction of the species and that it is of great interest as the majority of the species of the genus *Diploglosus* are ovoviviparous, which means that their eggs develop on the inside of the female and are not deposited on the outside so that the small lizard's newborns emerge to the outside world through the cloacal opening of the mother.

In Cuba there are two subspecies or geographical races: *Diploglossus delasagra delasagra* that is present in all of Cuba from Pinar del Rio to the northwest region of the province of Holguín and Isla de la Juventud and *D. d. nigropunctatus* own of the mountains of the eastern provinces. This species has often found in the surrounding coffee plantations to La Melba, Moa municipality, province of Holguín, using as a shelter the rotten wood of the numerous trunks of Najesí and other species which are scattered by the moist soil of the coffee plantations.

The diet of this species is not known in detail, since that has not been the subject of studies in our country, but we can refer to some data belonging to the diet of *D. warreni* from Dominican Republic and that is similar to our species. In the contents of the stomachs of more than 40 individuals surveyed scientists have found the following groups of invertebrates in quantities of more than 10 % of the total of the content: Chilopods (centipede 21 %); Diplopods (millipedes 15 %); cicadas (cicadas 15 %) and Arachnids (spiders and scorpions 11 %). The remaining 33% of stomach contents was composed by various groups of invertebrates, and small reptiles. The diet of the Four-legged Small Snake, could be very similar to the Dominican species, which devours large quantities of species that live in their habitat.

It has been our intention that this article has served so readers know a little more of our fauna of reptiles and also has helped to clarify the doubts about the identity of the Cuban Night Lizard (*Cricosaura typica*) and the Four-legged Small Snake *(Diploglossus delasagra)*.

15

Small Snake With Four Legs *Diploglossus delasagra* (Photo: A. R. Estrada)

Comments

Today Science recognizes three different species of Small Snakes With Four Legs. Subsequent to this publication, several Cuban - U.S. herpetological expeditions organized by the National Museum of Natural History of Cuba and partially funded the foreign part, allowed discover a new species of *Diploglossus* and consider races or subspecies of *D. delasagra* as two different species. The new species (*Diploglossus garridoi*) described in 1998 by Richard Thomas and S. Blair Hedges, was dedicated to the Cuban naturalist Orlando H. Garrido, known for his contributions to Ornithology, Herpetology and Entomology of Cuba. The remaining two species were named as *D. delasagra* and *D. nigropunctatus*. The species described in 1989 *D. garridoi*, is known in the vicinity of the type locality, El Manguito, Buey Arriba in Granma Province, on the northern slope of the Sierra Maestra, while *D. delasagra* is distributed in all of Cuba from Pinar del Rio to Camagüey.province. Meanwhile *D. nigropunctatus* is distributed in the eastern provinces of Holguín and Guantánamo.

Diploglossus garridoi (Photo: S. B. Hedges)

4 Little winged jewels of our islands

El precioso pajarito prefiere vivir en zonas bien forestadas, incluyendo cafetales y bosques de montaña, y en las tierras llanas prefieren los bosques secos como el de Guánica. La especie cubana se conoce como la Cartacuba o Pedorrera (Todus multicolor).

BIOLOGIA

Pequeñas joyas aladas de nuestras islas

Por ALBERTO R. ESTRADA
ESPECIAL PARA EL NUEVO DIA

SIN DUDAS una de las maravillas de la avifauna de Puerto Rico es el Sanpedrito, esa pequeña ave de apenas 11 cm (4.5") y de vivo colorido verde, amarillo y rojo. El Sanpedrito es una especie que vive solamente en tierra boricua, o sea que es tan genuinamente puertorriqueño como el coquí. Paradójicamente su nombre científico es *Todus mexicanus*, porque erróneamente los ejemplares que se usaron para describir la especie fueron considerados procedentes de México.

Excelentes cazadores

Especialmente en las mañanas soleadas se le puede ver muy activas procurándose su alimento. Los Sanpedritos son unos excelentes cazadores de insectores al vuelo. ¿Cómo lo hacen?, pues se colocan al

donde las podemos encontrar en abundancia. Su época de reproducción transcurre desde marzo hasta julio. Los Sanpedrito son pequeñísimas cavadores que usan las barrancas de caminos para construir una galería curva de unos 60 cm

> El Sanpedrito, especie que vive sólo en Puerto Rico, es excelente cazador de insectos al vuelo. Son muy poco tímidos y permiten acercárseles

territorio de alimentación y sus nidos, posible observar refulcas entre Sanpedri de diferentes parejas por un territorio caceria o porque una pareja comienze cavar un túnel en las inmediaciones nido de una pareja ya establecida, postura más habitual al posarse en u ramita, es con el pico erguido, dejando el color rojo de su garganta y de la pa inferior del pico.

Sólo en las Antillas Mayores

Esta joya de Puerto Rico pertenece a u familia de aves (Todidae) emparentada la del Martín Pescador. Las restantes cua especies conocidas viven sólo en

Published in the daily El Nuevo Dia (San Juan, Puerto Rico) on Sunday, December 27, 1998.

After emigrating from Cuba to the United States, I established in Puerto Rico, and between December 1998 and January 1999, and with the help of Mimi Ortiz, a journalist from the Puerto Rican newspaper El Nuevo Dia, had the opportunity to publish some articles in the Sunday section of science of that newspaper. The following is a work dedicated to a group of endemic birds of the Greater Antilles.

Undoubtedly, one of the wonders of the bird fauna of Puerto Rico is the Puerto Rican Tody, this small bird of just 11 cm (4.5 ") and bright colors of green, yellow and red. The Puerto Rican Tody is a species that lives only on Puerto Rican island, so it is as genuine as the Puerto Rican Coquí. Paradoxically, its scientific name is *Todus mexicanus*, because wrongly the specimens that were used to describe the species were seen coming from Mexico.

These tiny winged creatures, living in almost all types of forests that are still in our island, and are truly hard to find amid the foliage of vegetation, thanks to the Green predominating in their plumage. Little shy birds, are since it is possible to approach a few steps, so close that it might seem to us that we can almost touch it. It is easier to locate these birds, through by their voice, that if you try to look for them with his eyes look. A simple *chueep* or a double *chueep-chueep*, also produce a kind of buzz by flapping its wings.

Excellent hunters

Especially on sunny mornings you can be very active trying their food. The Puerto Rican Tody is an excellent flight-catchers of the insects. How can it do? Tody sits on the lookout from a twig, scanning their environment waiting for prey fly near or at least flutters in foliage above its position and then with a surprisingly quick flight, trap the prey with its beak and back to the twig and swallow their food with incredible skill, and start a new stalking.

Very small diggers

Prefer to live in well forested areas, including mountain forests and coffee plantations, and in the plain lands prefer dry forests like Guánica, where we can find them in abundance. Its breeding season runs from March to July. The Puerto Rican Tody are tiny diggers, which used the ravines of roads to build a curved gallery of about 60 cm (two feet) which ends in a small cavity where lay one to four white eggs. Do not cover the nest with any other material. Both the male and female participate in the construction of the nest by turns. Sometimes the young children of the past year help in the care of the new chicks at the new nest, which reinforces the successful reproduction of the species.

They defend their territory

The Puerto Rican Todies are very territorial birds who actively defend their territory of power and their nests. Regularly occur conflicts and clashes between different pairs for a territory of hunting Todies or because a couple begins to dig a tunnel in the vicinity of the nest of another already established couple. They have a peculiar way of perching on a twig, with its beak pointing up and revealing the red throat and lower beak.

Only on the Greater Antilles

This jewel of Puerto Rico belongs to a family of birds Todidae related Kingfisher. The remaining four known species live only in the Greater Antilles. Cuba and Jamaica have a unique species each, such as Puerto Rico and Hispaniola has two. Cuban species is known as the Cartacuba (*Todus multicolor*) Cuban Tody, the Jamaican species as Jamaican Tody (*Todus todus*) and the species of Hispaniola is named Broad-billed Tody (*Todus subulatus*) and Narrow-billed Tody (*Todus angustirostris*) respectively. All Todies closely resemble each other and there are only slight differences of color, voice and size. But all are a legitimate product of the West Indian nature.

Narrow-billed Tody (*Todus angustirostris*) [Photo: A. R. Estrada]

Broad-billed Tody (*Todus subulatus*)[Photo: A. R. Estrada

Cuban Tody (*Todus multicolor*) [Photo: A. R. Estrada]

Puerto Rican Tody (*Todus mexicanus*) [Photo: A. R. Estrada]

5 The anole lizards of the West Indies

Published in the daily El Nuevo Dia (San Juan, Puerto Rico) on Sunday, January 7, 1999.

In my early days as a field biologist the anole lizards were protagonists at some of my research in Cuba. I had the opportunity to publish several scientific articles on population ecology of some species and the good fortune to discover and describe new species for science.

The second of my contributions from popular science for El Nuevo Día, is about this group of lizards.

Perhaps for our audience, which in these times has been subjected to the spectacle of the films of science fiction about resurrected dinosaurs, or countless documentaries for TV about the large mammals that inhabit the savannahs and jungles of Africa, Asia, South America and Australia; the most common belief is that the fauna of our West Indian Islands is irrelevant or simply devoid of interest It is true that our small islands do not have those creatures, but instead other groups of very special animals still survive in our battered environments. The lizards of the genus *Anolis*, are one of those prices provided to us by the local nature.

Puerto Rico has 13 species

These reptiles are small usually (five and 18 cm in total length) belong to family of the iguanids are unique in the Americas and are found from the South of the United States to Patagonia in South America, and the West Indies. More than 300 species are known and 146 of them living on the islands of the Caribbean Sea. The archipelagos of greater diversity of anoles of the West Indies are Cuba (56 species) and Hispaniola (43 species). Puerto Rico has 13 of these species that are endemic to the Puerto Rican archipelago, and some of them are exclusive species of several of our small islands like the Mona Anole (*Anolis monensis*) and Desecheo Anole (*Anolis desechensis*).

Change their coloration

In the majority of species of anole, there is a marked difference between males and females. Males are usually larger in size and possess a fold of skin in their throat known as dewlap that almost always has bright colors. Sexually active males displayed the dewlap made a series of elaborate body movement like push-ups and vertical balancing of the head. They do this to get noticed by the females and other males. Another interesting feature of the anoles is the change of their coloration. This property makes them take colors that blend with the substrate on which they are.

Unbelievable diversification.

Anole lizards have been the product of an incredible diversification of forms that they have allowed them to adapt to the most varied environments and types of habitats, we find them in all kinds of forests, from the dry plain and coastal areas and to the more humid forests like the dwarf forest of the higher levels of the anvil. Also every kind of forest include species that have developed special adaptations that allow them to exploit resources more varied, so have lizards whose body shape enables them to move with incredible dexterity and agility between weed them and crawling ferns in the Woods. Their bodies are slim as sticks; they are equipped with long hind legs and a long tail, its peculiar Anatomy enables them to navigate through incredible precision jumps. Two species of this type are the gardener's Puerto Rico lizard (*Anolis pulchellus*), and the stick of the Escambray in Cuba lizard (*A. vanidicus*). We can also find species adapted to live in the forests of the banks of the rivers, with a high capacity for swimming and diving. It is the case of a Cuban species known as alligator lizard (*Anolis vermiculatus*).

Crested Anole (*Anolis cristatelus*) [Photo: A. R. Estrada)

Can camouflage itself with its habitat.

Other species as the common crested Puerto Rico lizard (*Anolis cristatelus*), can be found on the trunks and the ground of the trees and shrubs of varied types of forests or in the gardens of the areas transformed by development. The case of another Puerto Rican species: the hidden lizard (*Anolis ocultus*) is an example of near-perfect adaptation to life in the fine twigs of the foliage of the trees at the highest levels of the tropical forest, its color and the shape of your body with short legs allow you to confused with fine twigs which seeks its food and evade predators in their habitat. Its main natural enemies are nocturnal and diurnal birds of prey, crows, silly birds and snakes.

Important predators.

The anoles are important predators of insects, and in most of the species more than 60% of its diet is made up of different species of ants, about 20% are beetles, and other diverse groups of insects and spiders make up the rest. This function of eating insects is not exclusive of the anoles; other diurnal reptiles also consume insects. Amphibians and other nocturnal reptiles as some snakes and bats are in charge of this task during the night. As most reptiles reproduce by eggs females deposited in various places such as between the leaf litter on the forest floor; in a hollow of a tree trunk; between the mosses; or on the ground. Some species tend to lay their eggs in communal sites, which means that in breeding season several females select the same spot to lay their eggs.

Giant Anoles

Some species of anole lizards are known as Giant Anoles; this group of species reaches sizes that can exceed 30 cm from the tip of the snout to the end of the tail. The giant anoles are often found at the top of the trees of the dense forests and can be included in your diet, snails, and small birds. Despite living on top of the forest canopy they tend to descend in the hottest hours of the day, between 11:00 am and 1:00 pm, in these times you can discover them on the trunks and very close to the ground. Eventually many of these species feed on the ground, where they also lay their eggs. Puerto Rico has two of these giant species: *Anolis cuvieri* and *A. roosevelti*. The Giant Anole group is present in the Hispaniola but is in the Cuban archipelago where giant anoles had its greatest diversification with seven species. The Cuban species are somewhat larger in size than their cousins from Hispaniola and Puerto Rico.

Puerto Rican Giant Anole (*Anolis cuvieri*) [Photo: A. R. Estrada]

Very vulnerable

Some of the species of the Caribbean Islands clutch live in confined spaces, adapted to very special conditions in unique habitats. These characteristics make them particularly vulnerable to dramatic transformations of the environment. The devastation of some natural areas to the thrust of the socio-economic development, the flawed forest management, and the introduction of exotic species, are some of the causes that can cause the extinction of some of our exclusive lizards, as it is the case of the Giant Anole of the islands of Culebra and Saint Croix *A. roosevelti* in serious danger of extinction due to habitat loss.

Olive Bush Anole (*Anolis krugi*) [Photo: A. R. Estrada

Comments

Fifteen years after published the previous article, the number of species under the genus *Anolis* has increased and also the considerations on the family name and the taxonomic treatment of some species of other genera of anoles, now included under the genus *Anolis*.

The total number of species of *Anolis* today estimated at 390 and to the region of the Antilles is 161 species.

Namely, 13 species of Puerto Rico, to which must be added: three species of the Virgin Islands, 25 species in the Lesser Antilles, four in the Cayman Islands, six in Jamaica, four great Bahama Bank, 42 species Hispaniola Island and 64 species of the archipelago of Cuba.

The quantities of species by groups of Islands or archipelagos do not include species introduced into an archipelago or shared, only the native. The phylogenetic relationships of Anoles lizards, their classification and their inclusion in one family or another, remains a controversial topic, the author prefers to follow the approach of those who still consider these lizards as iguanids.

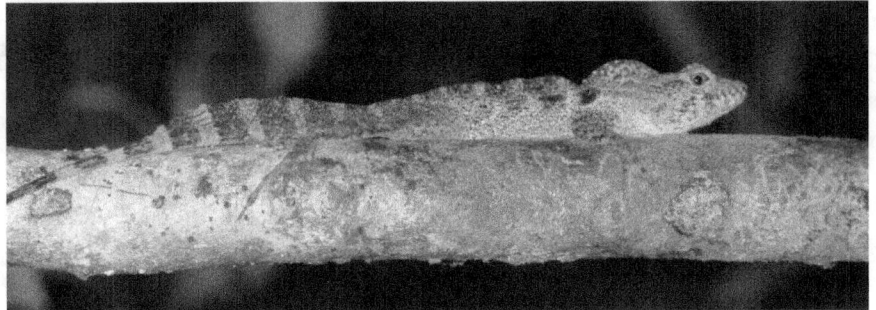

Yellow-chinned Anole (*Anolis gundlachi*) [Photo: A. R. Estrada]

Mona Anole (*Anolis monensis*) [Photo: A. R. Estrada]

6 The extinction of the Ivory-billed Woodpecker in Cuba

126 BIOLOGIA — CIENCIA — EL NUEVO DIA-DOMINGO 10 DE ENERO DE 1999

La reciente extinción del carpintero real

POR ALBERTO R. ESTRADA
ESPECIAL PARA EL NUEVO DIA

CUANDO PENSAMOS en la extinción casi siempre viene a nuestra memoria la famosa extinción de los Dinosaurios, que según las últimas hipótesis de los científicos se relaciona con el impacto de un fabuloso meteorito que produjo un verdadero desastre planetario. Pero la extinción además, de ser un fenómeno natural, en la mayoría de los casos más recientes se debe a la propia acción de la humanidad que como una lluvia incesante de meteoritos extirpa especies de animales y plantas de nuestro planeta a un ritmo difícil de imaginar.

Algunos expertos han señalado como ejemplo que en la primera mitad del presente siglo la actividad transformadora de la naturaleza desarrollada por la humanidad produjo la extinción de al menos una especie de ave y una especie de mamífero. Como fácilmente podemos imaginar este ritmo debe haberse incrementado notablemente en nuestros días de las postrimerías de esta centuria.

La más espectacular de las especies de pájaros carpinteros que haya vivido en tierras antillanas habitó en Cuba hasta hace apenas 10 años

Published in the daily El Nuevo Dia (San Juan, Puerto Rico) on Sunday, January 10, 1999.

One of the most important events in my career as a biologist, was undoubtedly the see me involved with my colleague and friend, Giraldo Alayón García, in the preparation of a project to establish the status of conservation of spectacular Ivory -billed Woodpeckers, which since the mid-20th century had seen for the last time in the intricate mountains of the eastern region of Cuba.

This article reviews the results of those expeditions.

When we think of the extinction almost always comes to our memory the famous extinction of the dinosaurs, which according to the latest hypothesis scientists relates to the impact of a fabulous meteorite that produced a true planetary disaster. But extinction is a natural phenomenon, but in most of the more recent cases, is due to the destructive action of mankind on ecosystems, which like a ceaseless rain of meteorites, removed species of animals and plants of our planet at an unimaginable rate.

Some experts have pointed out as an example that in the first half of the 20th century the transforming activity of nature developed by mankind produced the extinction of at least one species of bird and one species of mammal per year. As we can easily imagine this rate should have increased significantly in our days of the aftermath of this century.

The most spectacular of all the species of woodpeckers of the West Indies

Today our protagonist is not a local species (not because our escape to the extinction process), but because it is the most spectacular species of woodpeckers who has lived in West Indian lands: the Ivory-billed Woodpecker that lived in Cuba until just 10 years ago.

Campephilus principalis is its scientific name and in addition to Cuba lived in the forests of southern Louisiana and Florida where it became extinct for more than 30 years ago. Its size was more than 19 inches from the tip of the beak to tail end, and its wingspan exceeded 17 inches. Males exhibited a tuft of red feathers on the nape and their plumage is highlighted by its color black and furrowed by a white stripe on its back and along wings, females have the plume or crest of feathers on the head black.

This species lived in vast areas of tropical forest that existed on the island of Cuba and that began to disappear in an extensive manner in the mid-nineteenth century, with the development of the sugar industry. Already in 1868 the German naturalist Johannes Gundlach (father of the Cuban Zoology) had referred to the disappearance of large areas of forests and the presence of residual populations of Ivory-billed Woodpecker in remote areas of the Cuban territory.

Almost a century later...

More than 100 years after the reports of Gundlach announced the beginning of the extinction of this species, a group of Cuban, American and Netherlander scientists, joined forces to clarify the status of the species. Following the track of the last sightings of these birds in 1956, a group of Cuban biologists achieved a couple of sightings between 13 and 16 of March 1986 in the remote region of Ojito de Agua, lost in the entrails of the mountain ranges of Moa in the eastern region of Cuba.

Lester L. Short, Jennifer Horne and George Reynard in April 1986, also achieve several sightings in the same region. A couple of Cuban biologists achieve another sighting near Ojito de Agua in March 1987.

After that, more than one dozens of national and international expeditions, were organized, but no new sightings in this remote territory covered by the last natural pine forest in that region were achieved.

The different expeditions established numerous hypothesis based on the sightings reported in the region of Moa in 1956 and the most recent 1986 and 1987. Almost all raised existence of a small number of individuals of the species caught in an area no larger than 72 square miles and its possible move to other areas to the west and east through narrow corridors of vegetation along the canyon of the rivers Jaguaní and Toa whose sources are born in the vicinity of Ojito de Agua.

Part of the evidence provided by the expeditions are concerned certain visible traces on dead pine trees that were identified as the work of the peak of these birds in their search for food (worms, and larvae of beetles that feed on dead wood). These marks were nothing but wide rings of bark removal of dead pines.

Between 1985 and 1987 a brigade of the forestry Forest Enterprise Guantánamo extracted thousand cubic feet of pine bolus for railway sleepers. Paradoxically these workers acted as guides and hosts for Cuban and Cuban-American expeditions March and April 1986. Additionally, 1989 and 1991 of part of the pine forest of Ojito de Agua suffered a fire that destroyed a valuable part of the forest, although many of these trees became potential food sources for the ivory-billed, providing a livelihood for many species of beetles and other insects whose larvae eat dead wood.

Seven years after the sightings of March and April of 1986 a team of biologists from Cuba and Netherland explored the regions of Ojito de Agua, Cupeyal del Norte, Peak Toldo, Yarey Mine, and Monte Iberia, did not find the expected existence patches virgin forests enough to provide logs of an appropriate size, capable of providing shelters and nests for Ivory-billed Woodpecker. Each remote corner within the area virtually occupied by birds sighted was thoroughly revised without locate a single vestige of a hole built by this species.

A perfect imitations of the call of the species were widespread in the region through a nozzle especially prepared for this purpose, this call is heard in several hundred meters away and it was never obtained a response, or it was sighted any Ivory-billed Woodpecker after more than 1,300 hours of observation.

Witnesses of the extinction

Unfortunately, these expeditions attended the final moment of a long process of extinction mainly caused by a dramatic disappearance of the natural habitat of this species: tropical forests with high diversity of species of hardwood and softwood (such as pines). These latter species are very important as they used to build their homes inside hollow logs or dead specimens of pine 20-30 meters high.

The loss of natural habitat continues to carry other species in the whole environment of the Antilles to extinction: birds, terrestrial and marine mammals, amphibians and reptiles, butterflies, palm trees, orchids, corals and fish. New rumors of sightings of the Ivory-billed Woodpecker is still heard in some coffee plantation in eastern Cuba, but scientists know that this jewel of West Indian wildlife departed forever.

Comments

In 2004 a group of ornithologists led by the Cornell Lab of Ornithology reported sightings of at least one male Ivory-billed Woodpecker in a region called Big Woods in the Momroe County, Arkansas. The report was published on April 28, 2005 in the journal Science. The sighting had occurred on 11 February 2004. During the 14 months following the sighting, a team of professionals sought with much insistence any evidence about the presence of the species in the Wildlife Refuge of the White River. In that period at least seven alleged sightings of the same individual were recorded.

On April 25, 2005 the team was able to record a video of low-resolution of a presumed Ivory-billed Woodpecker. The distribution of black and white plumage on its back and wings, was used as evidence that the bird was an Ivory-billed Woodpecker. The team of researchers also reported hearing repeatedly the typical sound of drumming from its peak. Later in July 2005, new recordings, reinforce the results pointing a rediscovery of the species in the United States.

The Ivory-billed Woodpecker had been seen in the United States since 1940 and in Cuba since 1987. The International Union for Conservation of Nature, had declared the species extinct in 1994, but given the evidence provided decided to change their status and declare it as Critically Endangered.

7 The manatee Rafael, back to the sea

Published in the magazine Panorama of the Metropolitan University (San Juan, Puerto Rico) on September, 2004.

Although my work as a researcher of the fauna of Cuba I mostly related to studies related to amphibians, reptiles, and birds, certain circumstances led me, in the beginning of my working life, to participate in a project on the conservation of the Manatee in the Cuban archipelago

As part of this research, I established correspondence with many researchers studying manatee populations of Florida in the United States and other islands of the Antilles.

One of those colleagues was Antonio. A. Mignucci who had founded the Caribbean Stranding Network (CSN) in Puerto Rico. In 1994 I briefly visited Mignucci, which then operated the facilities of CSN in the Magueyes island at La Parguera, Lajas. So we began a long friendship and a fruitful collaboration in the field of the conservation of the Manatee in Puerto Rico.

On 9 November 1999 an orphan baby manatee, was rescued in Luquillo, by watchmen of the Department of Natural and Environmental Resources (DNER). Biologists and volunteers from the Laboratory of Marine Mammals of the Caribbean (LMMC) and the Caribbean Stranding Network (CSN), worked from the time of their rescue, to save his life. In the pools of rehabilitation of the LMMC of Metropolitan University, a large group of students of the careers in biology and environmental science with volunteers, advised by the biologists of the CSN, cared and fed to Rafael for 46 months. During his rehabilitation reached an approximate weight of 318 kg (700 lb.) and 2.5 meters (8.2 feet) in total length.

Rafael was trained to facilitate handling during veterinary examinations, once returned to their natural habitat. On 19 September 2003, The Manatee Rafael was transported to a marine pool, as a final stage for their total rehabilitation. In his last weeks in the LMMC, Rafael adapted to carry a belt at the base of the caudal peduncle, where a floating transmitter which aims to track the displacement of Rafael was connected. Number 592 tattooed on his back, identifies Rafael.

The Manatee was rigorously subjected to veterinary examinations every two weeks in the first month, and then every four weeks to monitor their State of health and their adaptation to saline environment. The tests provide information relevant envelope: general physical condition, their growth in length, weight, blood chemistry, bacteriology and urine.

On December 12, 2004 was the last of these veterinary checkups, and the results indicated that Rafael had stabilized their weight, and is was adapting well to feed if only in the environment of the marine pool. These results suggested that the date of opening the gate of the fence towards the total liberation was close. But surges that occurred between 19 and 22 December tore down the top of a section of the fence that delimits the pool on the beach of Punta Salinas, and in the early hours of Tuesday, December 23, Rafael left the place moving to Boca Vieja Cove, to the southeast of the pool. This early release tensed all staff of the CMML, which immediately began to track the movements of Rafael in the cove. With the help of the Argos Satellite System of telemetry tracking, and using a portable receiver on Earth, its position was located on the morning of the same December 23 close to the thermoelectric power plant of Palo Seco.

Rafael is adapted successfully to their lives in freedom, and continues to provide valuable information to researchers of the LMMC UMET, on the ecology and natural history of the species. Training behavior to which he was subjected, are already yielding fruits, providing veterinary tests that now practiced in shallow waters of the beaches of Boca Vieja Cove.

The LMMC will continue to follow closely from Rafael, and soon to be a transmitter to the Manatee Moses, that the CSN release almost 10 years ago in Ceiba, to study their current movements and compare them with those who were monitored after their release. Research on marine mammals, and other aspects of the ecology of estuaries and coastal environments is continuing its course, opening new opportunities to the student researchers from the Department of Science and Technology of the UMET.

Rafael the Manatee in his rehabilitation pool. (Photo: A. R. Estrada)

Training Rafael (Photos: CSN)

Comments

Rafael kept almost all the time in the vicinity of the mouths of the rivers Hondo and Bayamón in the waters of Boca Vieja Cove. After 14 months of having followed through radio telemetry system that it allowed to locate it by its transmitter signal, and after losing contact visual with the Manatee for several days, the signal from its satellite transmitter was located with some difficulty, stationary in the Bayamon River about 500 meters from the mouth.

A brief exploration of the banks of the River, allowed the CSN volunteers find the lifeless body of Rafael in February 2005.

Very close to where was found the body of Rafael, the CVR had rescued a baby abandoned manatee, Moses the Manatee, was rescued in November 1991, rehabilitated and returned to the sea in the Bay of Ceiba in 1994. Moses still live in the seas near Ceiba.

Another Manatee that was rescued in September 2005 in The Tuque, West of Ponce. The baby manatee nicknamed Tuque was also rehabilitated and then moved to Punta Salinas to the beach closed by a gate, where in 2004 Rafael was gradually adapted to live again in sea water.

Finally, Tuque was relocated in the region of the Natural Reserve of Jobos Bay in 2011.

Position of Rafael the Manatee at Boca Vieja Cove between December 29, 2003 and January 16, 2004.

Rafael in Punta Salinas (Photo: A. R. Estrada)

ABOUT THE AUTHOR

Alberto R. Estrada born in Havana, Cuba, where he studied Bachelor's degree in biological sciences with specialization in Vertebrate Zoology. He worked as a researcher in several centers in Cuba since 1982, until 1997. He was devoted to taxonomy and systemic of the amphibians and reptiles of Cuba. He has published over fifty articles in scientific journals of Cuba, Latin America, United States and Europe. He is also the author of several books. He lives in the United States since 1997.